Use Fewer Words

By Kevin Shinn

Photography by Kris Reiswig

55° Publishing

Lincoln, NE

55degrees.us

Introduction

To a painter, a canvas is an immediate limitation.

Choosing a form that is twelve inches by twelve inches means a boundary has been established. It dictates where the artist will paint. It doesn't tell the artist how to create the image. It only provides the perimeter.

The painter might choose to go all the way to the edges or stay within a select area on the board. But the picture will eventually emerge within that defined space.

I have chosen a similar limitation to express my writing.

I joined Twitter in June 2011 as a way to develop my writing skills. At that time, each message (tweet) could contain no more than 140 characters. The intention was to encourage brevity in communication. This limitation garnered my interest. As I started to use it, I saw how it prevented me from rambling; it provided welcome restraint.

Over time, I lost my initial interest in using Twitter as a platform for my written voice. Each time I opened the app, I was immediately hit with an overwhelming number of negative thoughts and opinions. I didn't like the way it made me feel anxious and agitated. So, I decided to discontinue using Twitter but wanted to see if I could find a way to keep writing in very short form.

Then I had an idea strike me out of nowhere.

I'd had an old Remington manual typewriter on a shelf in my basement for years. I'm not even sure where it came from or how I ended up with it. I pulled it down and set it on my desk to see if it still worked. I rolled in a sheet of paper and typed a few characters and saw that it was fully operational. Apart from replacing the ribbon and cleaning the dust off the keys with a puff of compressed air, it was ready to go.

In March 2020, I took a trip to Ireland and packed a book of Irish poetry recommended by a friend. I opened the work of John O'Donohue at the onset of a long train ride across the country and didn't get past the first five poems. I had never known poetry to have such a profound effect on my mind and emotions. I read those five poems many times during that excursion.

It made me wonder if my writing would ever have that kind of impact on anyone.

On April 3, 2020, I sat down at the typewriter on my desk

and tapped out a short quote from one of those poems. I took a photo of the words on the page in the carriage and posted it on my Instagram account.

My disappointment in myself was immediate. I looked at that post online. I knew I had made a mistake.

It was too safe.

As a writer, I knew intuitively that I needed to learn the courage to post my own work.

My heart knew the steps to take, even though I had never written poetry before, let alone share it with anyone. Nor would I ever know the joy of having my words matter to someone else.

I had to start writing and start sharing.

I began with what I knew: grief. I was a few months into my new life as a widower and was well acquainted with the unpredictable nature of grief that comes as a result of loss. Grief became my muse. I wrote what I felt, sometimes daily. As the practice continued, I found it easier for my mind to ponder complicated thoughts and express them in a short statement. It was a very powerful part of my grief process.

Through this project, I have found my goal in writing:

"I use my voice to help you hear yours."

I write in first person much of the time because I am writing advice to myself first. I am working out thoughts in my own life first. I believe if it makes sense to me, then it might make sense to someone else.

The title comes from one of my favorites:

To be a better writer

Be more honest

Tomorrow

Than you were today

And use fewer words.

I've taken this to heart in this project and tried to be as honest as I can and use as few words as possible. I hope you enjoy these short pieces. I hope they take on a life of their own in your heart.

On Writing

To be a better writer

Be more honest

Tomorrow

Than you were today

And use fewer words

Words want to be

Music

When they grow up

But they grieve

Because they know

Music doesn't require

Their services

Seek to find

Your voice

Not an audience

The audience

Will find you

If your voice

Is true

My name is writer

I find words

That sound like yours

If you read my words

And don't feel something

I've not done my job

My greater fear

Isn't that you would

Disagree with me

But that I would be

Misunderstood

I wrote a letter today

And as I sealed it

I imagined years from now

Someone finding it

In a drawer

And it made them cry

So, I wrote another letter

His words

Were like precious stones

He dug deep to find them

He faithfully bought them

To the surface

Only to be queried

Are these real

He continued to mine

His treasure

Until one day

The ore

Was fashioned

Into a dagger

And he dug no more

To never dig again

Would be safer

Knowing his words

Would not hurt anyone

And no one

Would misunderstand

But over time he realized

That no one had access

To his claim

No one but him

Would know where to dig

And no one would be encouraged

He would no longer

Offer hope

And feel the joy

Of placing his words

In your hands

And hear you say

Your words mean much to me

So he started digging again

Buried words

Are inert

Vacant and dormant

And the writer

Is their catalyst

I Can Still Hear Him Say

I can still hear him say

If you stop

Because you're tired

That's one thing

But if you stop

Because you're scared

That requires

A conversation

I can still hear him say

She was angry at God

And you were

The closest thing

That looked like him

And you washed

More than her feet

On defensive driving:

I can still hear him say

You might have the right of way

But you can be dead right too

I can still hear him say

Son, when you assume

You make an

Ass

Out of

U

And

Me

I can still hear him say

You may not be the guy

They ask

To captain the ship

But they will certainly

Find you

When the ship

Starts to sink

I can still hear him say

Allow the people

You dislike

To make you more curious

Than angry

I can still hear him say
Wash as low as possible
Wash as high as possible
Then wash your possible

I can still hear him say

Lots of folks

Are standing around

The edge

Waiting for someone

To jump in first

And they will most likely

Be looking

At you

I can still hear him say
Just because you can
Doesn't mean you should

I can still hear him say

The grass will come back

The boy won't

I can still hear him say

All that glitters

Is not gold

All that titters

Is not tit

I can still hear him say

Don't speak out

Against things

You don't understand

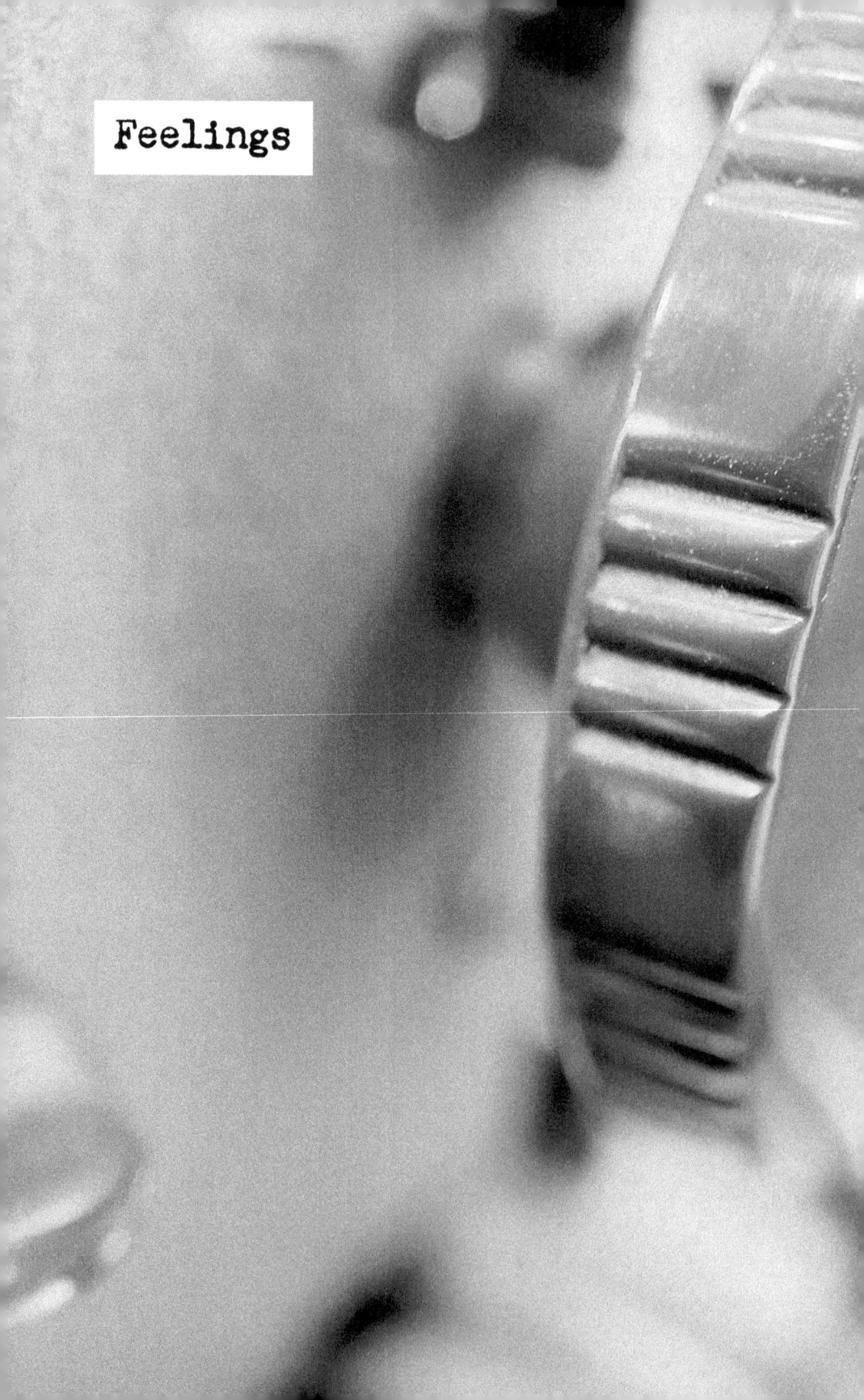

Feelings

You feel your way

Back to your heart

You don't think your way there

Someone

Who tells you

To get a grip

On your feelings

Probably has hers

In a stranglehold

Feelings are like caves

Deep

Dark

Spacious

A few spelunkers

Are fascinated by

What they find there

While the rest say

Can we get out of here now

Don't listen to your feelings
Said everyone
But wisdom insisted
Don't pay attention to that
It's bad advice

Wisdom continued
Never abandon your feelings
Just as you would never
Abandon a child
Listen intently to them
And like that child
Let them know they matter

Start by holding them
Close
As you would nurture
An infant
If you aren't sure what to do
I'll help you

Wisdom asked

Do you think I am void of feelings

I helped lay

The foundations

Of the earth

You think I didn't feel something

During that performance

A world without feelings

And the hearts that birth them

Would be dull and gray

That's not what I had in mind

Show me your feelings

Wisdom concluded

And I'll show you

How to paint

The most beautiful picture

In the world

When someone

Is reunited

With his feelings

After years of estrangement

Expect him to go overboard

Wholeness has that effect

When trying to reconnect

To your heart

Treat the first attempts

Like a blind date

Because your heart

Has felt unseen

For quite some time

When embarking

On a new journey in life

Don't worry about not knowing

Which way to go

A trustworthy guide

Will find you because

He will recognize

The lost look

On your face

Just say no

Is a perfect example

Of attempting to solve

A problem

While ignoring

The heart

Never be ashamed
To say you're in
A good place
Suffering
Isn't the point
Being alive is

The Body

The body told the heart
We were wounded
At the same time
By the same force
And that's when
You turned on me
The heart said
I'm so sorry

The body continued to speak
To the heart
Lead me to rest
There we can heal together
I can't rest
Until you do.

The heart asked the body
How do we heal together?
The body said

Listen to my stories
I've kept them all
Especially the ones
Where you hurt me

And the broken heart
Continued to show honor
And intently listen as
The broken body
Told its stories
And they soon
Felt the redress
Of their newfangled cooperation

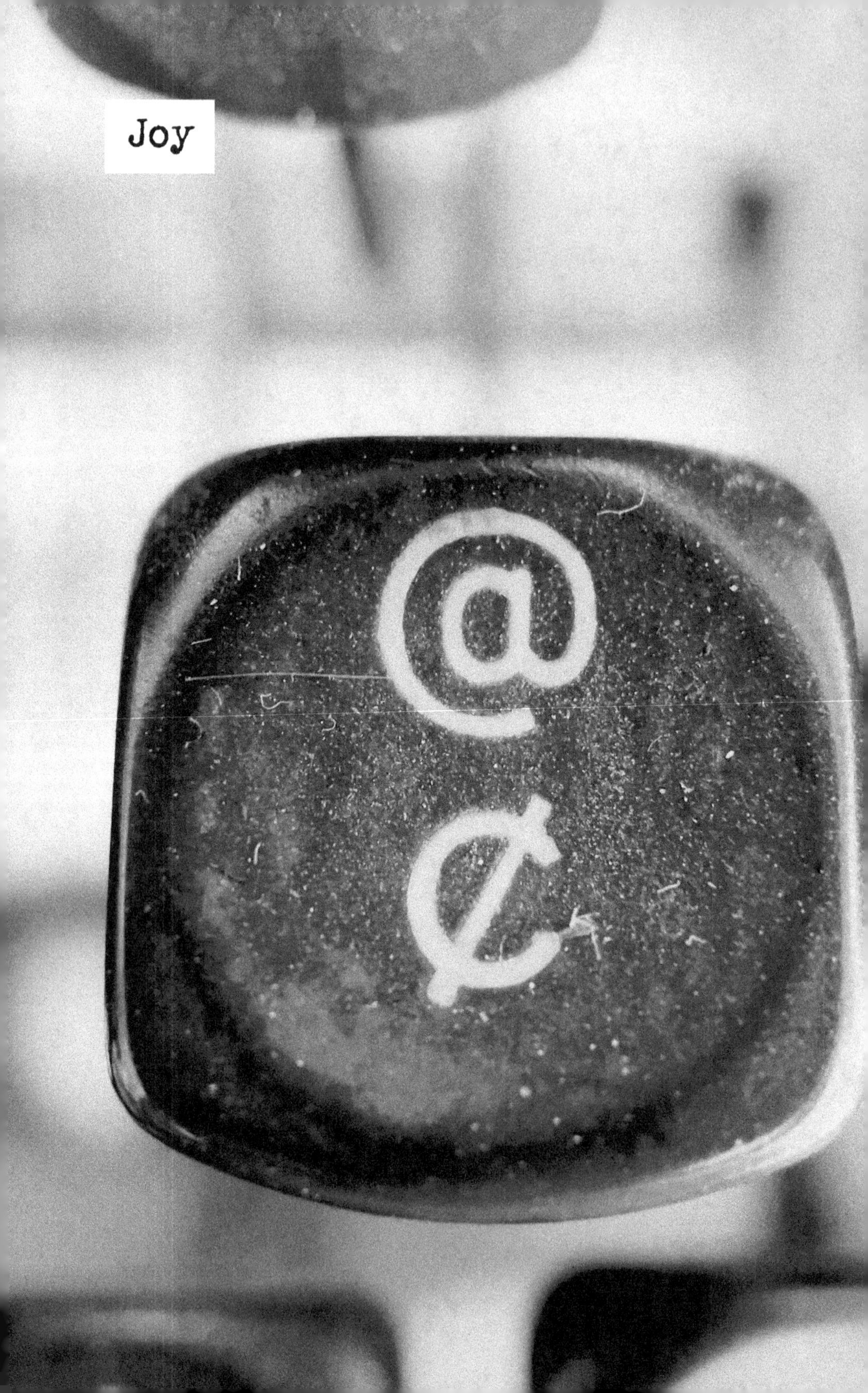

Joy

If you can't find

Your joy

No one stole it

Just retrace your steps

Till you find the place

Where you left it

Joy is like

That vase

You gave away

At the garage sale

You had no idea

Its value

Until it was gone

If you are running short

On joy

Find someone

Wealthy in it

They will give you so much

And without interest

Soon you will have more than

You can hold and

You will have to give it away

Share your joy

Freely with everyone

And don't be disappointed

If it doesn't get returned

The audience

Isn't your source

Hope is a bastard

Not born of us

It will undo our best work

Before we know it

So plant her seeds

And let the roots go deep

And become hard to pull

Or remove altogether

I started

Giving away

What I didn't get

And never had

Before long

I had plenty to give more away

Joy is a warrior princess

Fierce and tender

She will comfort you

And cut the balls off

Your worst enemy

Joy would never abandon me

But I've been known

To lose sight of her

Joy is too loyal

To leave me

But she is wise

To know when to be still

And let grief and pain

Have their say

Joy is a fascinating leader
She populates her entourage
With abundance

If you can't find abundance

Just look for joy

The two are inseparable

You will go out with joy

And the mountains will burst

With shouts of joy

That sounds like a

A pretty good date

Hope always waits

For you

In your future

No one needs hope

For what they already have

Hope and generosity

Make great lovers

When they rendezvous

More of each abound

Hope

Is the fiercest warrior

With the kindest voice

That will crush

The darkest opponent

And tuck your child in

At the end of the day

Anger likes to label

Hope as naïve

But she is too wise

To be offended

Anger is jealous

Of hope

Because she has

Better eyes

The fire of anger

Ignited by abuse

Exposes darkness

While hope

Takes the victims

By the hand

And moves to a safe place

When one stands

At the edge

Of the abyss

Looking down

Finding it contains

No solutions

Life can start to share

Her new secrets

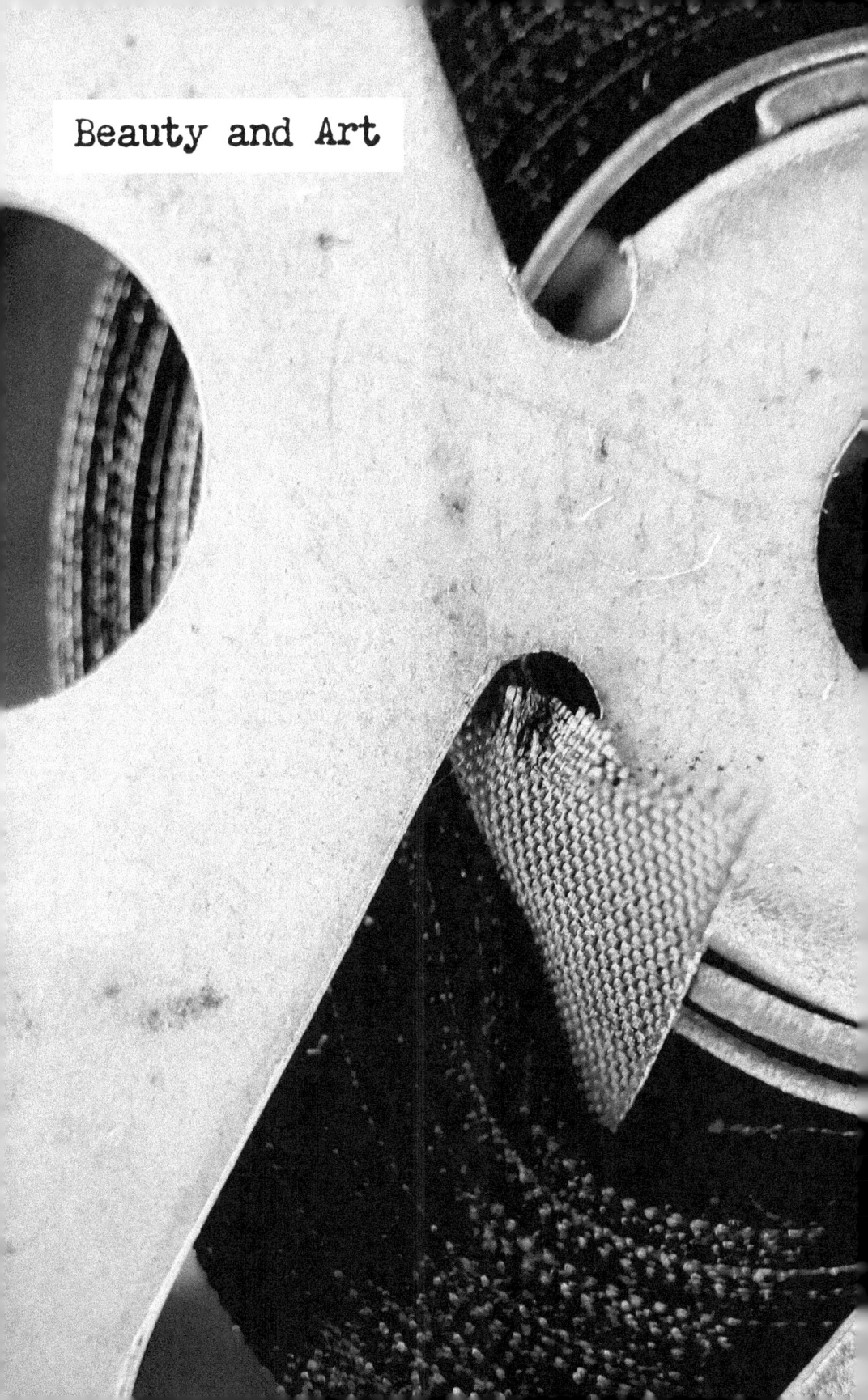

Beauty and Art

All beauty exists

To be adored

Even yours

Especially yours

Being seen

Is a natural part

Of being beloved

Why else

Would she wear

That beautiful dress

As she felt seen

And adored

Her armor melted

Like salt on ice

Nothing compares

To the ~~pain~~ joy

Of the mark

Inflicted by beauty

Upon the human heart

The moon teaches much

About the nature

Of beauty

Why else am I compelled

To stop

To gaze

Admire and sigh

Some days

The weight of beauty

Is too much to bear

But I would never suggest

She go on a diet

Beauty comes with a price
I can spend a fortune
Trying to keep it looking
The way it shouldn't

Beauty is my kryptonite

I buckle

Under her power

But it's a pretty good way

To go

Once she leaves

Her mark

Beauty

Is hard

To forget

Art is for the curious

Which is why many

Have no need for her

Don't expect art

To answer questions

Expect her

To raise more

The role of art

Is not to satisfy

She loves to reveal

Hunger

Art lives

For curious response

Even if the response is

What the hell is that

Good News

If it doesn't sound good

It isn't good news

If you hear him say

But first

Clean yourself up

Then it isn't good news

If you hear him say

But first

You need to change this

It isn't good news

Your father

Wants you

To come back home

That's good news

Any explanation

Of the good news

That includes

But...

Isn't good news

A union full of longing

Is free

Free to tussle

Free to yearn

Free to risk

Free to become

That's good news

When I say

I can't wait

For this to be over

It is translated

The good news

Doesn't apply

Right now

When I say

I can't wait

For this to be over

I continue to affirm

That the good news

Isn't that good

If you aren't free
It isn't truth

That's good news

As I sat by her bedside

I could feel death

Lurking in the room

And it wasn't long

To realize

That death doesn't travel alone

I knew the number of her days

Was nearing completion

And there was no way

I could prevent death

From completing its assignment

So I rested

A voice began to speak

Dictating how this experience

Would play out

Instead of attending to the instruction

I demanded silence

Then suddenly

Death's chief of staff
Exited the room

It was at that point
In the silence of that space
I discovered that death
Has no voice of its own
Death isn't permitted to speak
It can only steal
It was fear
Death's foremost principal
Who did all the talking

As death began to surround her body
I leaned in close
Close enough to smell the fetor
Of its withering breath
I spoke to it directly
Finish your assignment
And death couldn't say a word

When the announcement was made
That the number of her days was complete
Death was given its final permission
After it finished the singular task
It departed

I then found fear
Stared it down
And watched as it turned
And ran
In the same direction

After death left her room
I sat alone
At least I thought
A new voice appeared
Clear and unmistakable

I had just witnessed
The completion of her days

21,923 to be exact

And the Ancient of Days

Wanted to talk about it

Ancient means old

He reminded me

That he has been aware of this day

For a long, long time

Judging by his name

Days are important to him

So much so

That he asked me to number them

He promised if I did

I could cash it in

For a heart of wisdom

He reminded me

That he does not travel alone either

Out in front of his entourage

Is joy

And the leader of that pack
Is peace

Continue to number your days
And don't lose heart
He said
The best is yet to come

How you live

Is how you will leave

Live angry

Leave angry

Live happy

Leave happy

Live free

Leave free

Live forgiven

Leave forgiven

Anger

Anger

Is highly

Addictive

Anger without hope

Eyes without sight

Beauty without adoration

A living hell

Pain and anger

Are gifts

Never to be sought

But always to be opened

And the contents unpacked

If there is anger

In your voice

Remember this

Anger never leads to repentance

Kindness does

If my solution to a conflict

Involves dismissing

The party at odds

Then I've not solved anything

But instead

Created a new problem

Rend the heart
Of anger
Sunder it wide
Release the antigen
That has been mistaken
For nourishment

Injustice provokes anger

Anger provokes a respond

But love must always

Lead the way

Anger is only

A soldier

In the fight

Against injustice

Never promote it

To commander in chief

Beware the anger

Listen to it

Don't indulge it

Or become

Like the ones

I hate

Longing

When searching

For the voice of God

Find the kindest voice

In your head

And follow that one

To kill a longing

Is a sure

And certain way

To prevent the heart

From becoming whole

Longings

Are the fuel

That powers

The heart

Longings

Are not the problem

My tombstone

Will not read

He wanted too much

If being safe

Is the highest goal

Then

No one scales everest

No one reaches the moon

And no one falls in love

The easiest way

To avoid conflict

Is to not want anything

I clearly recall

The feeling at the edge

Of the abyss

It is why I will stand there

With you

And gently say

Don't jump

Be fully committed

To your pleasure

The kind that leads

To deep satisfaction

And not just

Immediate relief

I'm free to walk out

Of my prison

And I'm free

To stay put

And fondle my chains

Grief

All loss isn't equal

But all loss

Must be grieved

I grieved

Until I felt better

Then I realized

I've only gotten started

It's important

To distinguish

Between grief and loss

One shows up to help

The other to steal

When grieving

On some days

The best thing to do

Is to go ahead

And let someone else

Mow the yard

I didn't like grief

When we first met

I still don't like her

But I have new respect

For the importance

Of her work

In grief

Most tears

Will go unwitnessed

Grief will unlock

A door

To a room

Where you can go

To feel what you really feel

And not how someone else

Felt about her

Grief breeds honesty

It's not interested

In maintaining appearances

Or propping up

A hurtful past

Grief

Will lead me

Anywhere I want

And everywhere I don't

If you need me

You'll know where to find me

I'll be in the same place

I've always been

When it all started

To hit the fan

I dream of a day

When found

With tears in my eyes

I'm met with a smile

Instead of the question

What's wrong with you

It's been fifteen months
I still put the lid down

It's been fifteen months
I still make the bed
Every morning

It's been fifteen years
I still do all the cooking

When someone shares

About their loss

And you don't know

What to say

Don't

If someone says

I feel like killing myself

Never

Ever

Never ever say

You shouldn't feel that way

It's an invitation

Not a threat

Grab a flashlight

And gently enter their cave

To better grasp

The concept of faith

Observe someone

Who suffers well

Hang around people

Who know how to grieve

Before long

You might ask

Do I still need

These pills

Random Musings

use fewer words

Half a mile from nowhere
Took all day to get here
Got half a mind to turn around

My garden seeds

Arrived in the mail

Including a packet

For seedless watermelons

It was empty

Hang around people

Who laugh a lot

Before long

You won't have to ask

What's so funny

Hang around people

Who have been set free

Before long

You won't have to ask

Can we do this

Hang around people

Who are fully alive

Before long

You won't have to ask

What's my purpose in life

Hang around people

Who revel in the good

Of the good news

Before long

You'll start asking

What am I so mad about

Hang around people

Who are dumb enough

To believe

The good news

Is literally good

Before long

You'll wonder

What took me so long

If there is no peace

The wrong prince

Is in charge

I cleaned out my car

This afternoon

And found $7.38 in change

I should clean it out

More often

When I finally get around

To cleaning

The microwave

I should stop and ask

What else

Have I been ignoring

Prayer is not

The best response

In times of panic

Worship

Is far more effective

The best advice

For a cook

Is found in the dish pit

The dirty dishes

Will tell you

How well you did

That evening

The absence of argument

Is no indication

Of a good marriage

It could be a sign

That there is nothing worth fighting for